Life in MEDIEVAL ENGLAND 1066–1485

Rupert Willoughby

The castles, cathedrals and parish churches of England are the most impressive visible legacies of the Middle Ages. Almost all of them date from the period after 1066, when England was conquered by the Norman invaders from France. The buildings remain, but what of the life that went on inside them? For these were the haunts of the colourfully clad lords and ladies, the ribald clergymen and the servile peasants of popular legend. They were the backdrop to extravagant feasts, to tournaments between armoured knights, to courtly rituals, and to displays of fanatical piety. The colours may have faded, but the romance lingers still....

KINGS & COMMONERS

In 1066 the unified and prosperous England of the Anglo-Saxons was conquered by the invading Duke William of Normandy. Far from oppressing the natives for centuries, the Normans were quickly assimilated into English society. The Norman kings and the Angevins, or Plantagenets, who succeeded them, retained considerable possessions in France, so the French language and culture continued to be fashionable at the king's court, and among educated people generally. The natural language of almost everyone in medieval England, however, – including, in time, the king – was English; yet French survived for a long time in England as an official language. After 1066 English developed into a varied collection of dialects; northerners and southerners were unintelligible to each other at this time. A standard tongue was needed that could be understood by educated people throughout the country; and French, already an international language of culture, was well suited to the purpose.

The growth of a strong national identity in England began as early as the 13th century, and

Above: *Rochester Castle in Kent, founded soon after 1066 as a means of controlling the river Medway. The Norman word for a keep such as this was* donjon, *the origin of the word dungeon.*

the patriotic feeling generated in the 14th and 15th centuries by the Hundred Years War against France finally put paid to the official status of the French language, when Henry V, the victor of Agincourt in 1415, symbolically began to compose his campaign reports in English.

Above: *Edward I (1272–1307) in Parliament.*

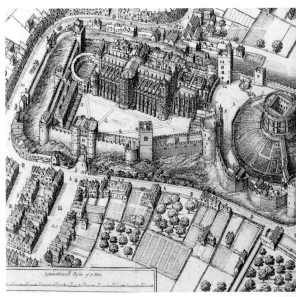

Another major effect of the Norman Conquest was the introduction of 'feudalism'. In a feudal society, every man or woman who held land did so in return for 'services' or obligations which were owed to a superior lord (the term 'landlord' originates from this arrangement). Feudal services usually consisted of a regular supply of troops and a pledge of loyalty. The king's closest companions, whether knights or clergymen, held vast estates. Parts of these were sub-divided among lesser knights, who might then distribute further portions of land among their own followers.

The mass of the population were peasants and worked on their lords' estates, farming the land and tending the livestock. A peasant who was legally free might be called upon to plough his lord's fields for 20 days each year. About 60 per cent of the peasants, however, were serfs or villeins (villagers), and were the property of their lord, who could buy and sell them as he pleased, and could call upon their labour at any time.

Below: The great keep at Windsor, the Round Tower. The mounds on which such fortifications were built were often man-made, and the earliest keeps were of wood.

Above: The coronation of Richard II (1377–99) took place when he was only 10 years old. This painting, in Westminster Abbey, is the earliest known portrait of a medieval king.

Left: Windsor Castle, Berkshire. Windsor, with its motte, or tower on a high mound, and bailey, the defensive courtyard below, is a typical medieval castle, although it was heavily restored in the 19th century.

The inequalities of the time were justified by the belief that the hierarchy of men was ordained by God. People did not always fit neatly into these categories: there were growing numbers of merchants, for example, who became wealthy on the profits of the wool and cloth trade. A successful merchant could aspire to social equality with a knight. Some merchants, like Dick Whittington, were themselves from noble families. Geoffrey Boleyn, Lord Mayor of London in 1457–58, married the daughter of a baron, and their great-granddaughter, Anne Boleyn, was to become Queen of England.

BARONS & KNIGHTS

Next in rank to the king in medieval society were the barons, including a handful of earls. These powerful and wealthy men were the king's tenants-in-chief, controlling large armies of knights loyal to their lord and the king. The first dukedoms were created in the 14th century, for the sons of Edward III, and there were no marquesses or viscounts in England until the 14th and 15th centuries. Through most of the medieval period, great men were content to be known by their own names and referred to as 'my lord', without the need for fussy titles and forms of address.

Although many prominent baronial families were wiped out during the Wars of the Roses (1455–85), some still flourish today. Their ancestors came from France in some cases but others are of English origin. Some are still represented in the House of Lords: this began in the Middle Ages as the Great Council, or Parliament, of the king, which it was the right of all barons to attend. The first 'commoners' to be summoned to this Parliament were representatives of the shires and boroughs and the lower clergy, whose approval of general taxes was considered, from the 13th century onwards, to be expedient, for the sake of

Above: *A 14th-century illustration showing William the Conqueror as the slayer of King Harold at the battle of Hastings.*

Left: *Portraits in stained glass of four prominent 14th-century barons, from a window in Tewkesbury Abbey, Gloucestershire. All four knights are wearing plate armour with heraldic surcoats, or 'coats of arms'.*

Right: *William the Conqueror (1066–87) portrayed as a medieval knight. The illustration dates from about 1321.*

effective government. Seven centuries and many bitter struggles later, the House of Commons has come to be the predominant legislative and governing body of the land.

Below the barons in rank were the few thousand members of the knightly class or gentry, whose representatives in the Commons were described as 'knights of the shire'. At the time of the Norman Conquest, knighthood was associated less with nobility than with violence and terror: the Anglo-Saxon word *cnihtas* means simply a youth or retainer, which was a precise enough description of the majority of the invaders. By the 13th century, however, it was almost exclusively the sons of noble families who were admitted to the order of knighthood. To be worthy of the rank, moreover, a knight was now expected to observe a strict code of honour and virtue – the so-called code of chivalry.

These developments coincided with the period of the Crusades, when enormous sacrifices were made by the knights of Western Europe in the cause of liberating the Holy Land from the Saracens, as their Muslim enemies were known. At the same time, owing to technical advances in warfare, the training and equipping of a knight had become a prolonged and extremely costly business; boys who were not born to wealthy backgrounds were

Above: *Every knight and baron was foremost a soldier – the necessary skills required years of training. This early 15th-century battle scene shows the plate armour which, by that time, had replaced the traditional suits of mail.*

inevitably excluded. Knights had thus come to regard themselves as an élite brotherhood. The poorer gentry were content to perform a no less vital role, though, by filling the offices of local government.

Below: *A 14th-century illustration from a history of the First Crusade. A Christian lord receives the key to a besieged city from a traitor within.*

PLOUGHING & REAPING

The majority of the population of about two million in medieval England could properly be described as peasants (countrymen). Their fortunes varied considerably, though, from the most prosperous freemen or franklins (like the one described in Chaucer's *Canterbury Tales*), who ranked immediately below the gentry and were the forerunners of the yeomen of later centuries, to the humblest serfs or cottars (cottagers) who laboured in conditions of considerable poverty and oppression.

The serfs, or villeins, were theoretically incapable of owning property, since they themselves were the chattels of their lords. One particularly vicious lord, the Abbot of Burton in Staffordshire, was charged in 1280 with the crime of robbing some of his villeins. In his defence, he argued that he had only taken what already belonged to him, since villeins were not entitled to own anything except their bellies. Moreover, the tenancies of the villeins were subject not to the common law of the land, but to the jurisdiction of the lords themselves in their own manorial courts.

Fortunately for the villeins, the traditional 'custom of the manor' dictated that the son of a deceased tenant would be able to 'inherit' his father's land by payment of a fine. He must also hand over a heriot, or death duties, which usually took the form of his best beast or other most valuable possession. It was in the lord's interest to ensure continuity on his estate, and its prosperity depended on a well-motivated peasantry. Provided their dues were paid, and their obligations met, many villeins were unlikely, therefore, to have

suffered more than occasional interference from their lords and masters.

The mere payment of a fine, for example, might enable a peasant to marry outside his own manor, to travel abroad on a pilgrimage (St James of Compostella, in northern Spain, was a popular destination), or to dispose of his property by means of a will. There is evidence that some peasants were extremely well-to-do (their grandsons or great-grandsons might well have found themselves in a position to take up knighthood) and that others were highly mobile. Except with regard to his tenancy or to minor offences, a villein was also entitled to the protection of the common law (as applied in the royal courts) against any injury to his person, even by his lord; he was therefore far from being a slave or chattel in the true sense.

Above: *Peasants lived and worked in harmony with the seasons.*

Below: *Livestock being fed with acorns which are felled from the trees.*

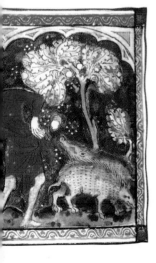

For the ambitious peasant, there were opportunities for considerable advancement in the boroughs or in the Church. A villein who wished to educate his son, to buy him an apprenticeship or have him admitted to the priesthood, had merely to pay a fine to his lord, in order to open up for him the possibility of a great career. One of the most renowned scholars and clerics of medieval England, Robert Grosseteste, Bishop of Lincoln (died 1253), was a villein's son.

Above: *Peasants at work hoeing and pruning in a vineyard.*

Below: *These illustrations show peasants sowing, ploughing and harvesting. Women were not excluded from the strenuous work.*

BISHOPS, ABBOTS & MONKS

To medieval Christians, a life of self-denial in a monastery seemed like the surest route to Heaven. The numerous monastic buildings that have survived in England, including some spectacular ruins, bear witness to the immense popularity, wealth and prestige of the medieval monasteries, which Henry VIII was to dissolve in the 1530s.

Many of the great cathedral churches in medieval England were the centres of monastic communities, the physical remains of which can still be glimpsed at such places as Canterbury and Westminster. The monastic atmosphere seems to linger in the quiet of many a cathedral precinct or 'close', such as those at Winchester and Rochester.

Most monasteries in England were obedient to the rule of St Benedict, a monk who, in 6th-century Italy, had devised a very strictly

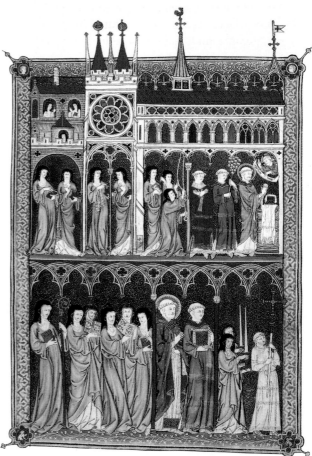

Above: *Nuns and priests shown in procession, below, and attending Mass, above. Life in the medieval monasteries observed strict rituals of prayer throughout the day and night. This illustration dates from the late 13th century.*

Above: *Pilgrims worshipping at the shrine of St Thomas Becket in Canterbury Cathedral. Every great church and monastery had a number of holy relics. The pilgrims who visited them were promised the remission of some of their sins.*

disciplined routine of labour and prayer. However, monasteries like Battle Abbey, founded by William the Conqueror on the battlefield of Hastings, had been endowed with vast estates. Since they were responsible for the management of these estates and the wealth that they created, the monks were inevitably much distracted by worldly matters. Bishops and abbots (the heads of monasteries) were treated no differently from ordinary landowners, and, indeed, were in every way the equals of the barons, attending the councils of the king, serving in his government, and returning feudal services for their lands.

The foundation of the Cistercian Order was an attempt to return to the purer form of religious life. The favourite retreats of these 'White Monks' were in remote, underpopulated regions, as far as possible from human habitation. In 1132, one group founded the famous abbey of Rievaulx in a desolate part of north Yorkshire. They were soon followed by a party of discontented Benedictines from York, who settled on waste land in Skeldale. From a collection of huts beneath an elm tree, these men were to build the Abbey of St Mary of Fountains, perhaps the most famous of all Cistercian monasteries. The aim of these monks was not only to be self-sufficient but also to be free from the problems of dependent tenants.

These ideals were to be thwarted, however, by the Cistercians' skilful exploitation of the lands

Right: *Medieval monasteries were centres of scholarship and produced some of the greatest writers of the period. This 12th-century illustration shows Eadwine, a monk at Canterbury.*

around them, which proved to be ideal pasturage for sheep. Within a century, the Cistercian Order had become England's leading producer of wool, at a time when the wool trade was the source of half the nation's wealth. The magnificent buildings that survive at Fountains and Rievaulx are testimony to the enormous profits that were made.

Unfortunately, they did not escape the attention of the government. In 1194, when a huge ransom had to be raised for the release of Richard the Lionheart from his captivity in Germany, the seizure of the Cistercians' entire wool crop for that year went a long way towards paying it. By that time, sadly, the Cistercians had already become a by-word for avarice.

Above: *A detail from the famous Winchester Bible, in the chained library in Winchester Cathedral. The illuminated manuscripts produced in monasteries are superb works of art.*

Right: *Rievaulx Abbey, in North Yorkshire, was built in a remote area by the Cistercians, who were attempting to withdraw from the world.*

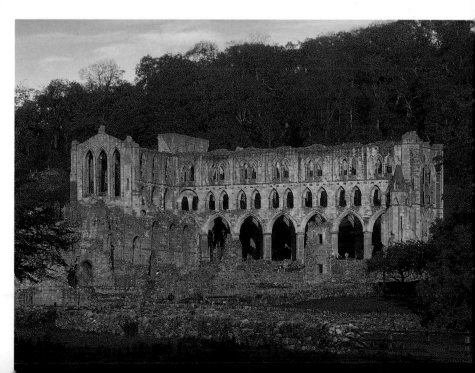

CASTLES & COTTAGES

Many houses and castles of the rich and powerful survive from the Middle Ages, including those of merchants (Stokesay), bishops (Rochester Castle and Acton Burnell), and mighty barons (Warwick Castle). The essential features of these dwellings were the great hall, a barn-like room, usually at least two storeys high, with a central hearth, which was the principal gathering-place of the castle or manor; a great chamber (often on an upper floor, and therefore called a *solar*, from the French word for a floor or beam), which provided the lord and his family with a more private retreat; and a domestic chapel or oratory, where the lord would attend daily prayers with his resident chaplain. Very often there would be more than one great chamber and chapel, and some lesser halls as well. There would usually be a kitchen and buttery leading off from the hall.

Unlike today, the life of medieval people was communal, and no-one would have expected to live alone. Peasant families might run their small-holdings as co-operatives. Young people of all classes would be boarded in other households, to act as servants and to receive some sort of training, whether as craftsmen or in the skills of knight-hood. Noblemen would attract large numbers of such people, as well as their own nephews and cousins and the landless younger sons of other

Right: A tiny oratory, or chapel, in a turret of St Thomas's Tower at the Tower of London, adjoining a hall and chamber built by Edward I in the 1270s. It would have been richly painted.

noble families, who became the lords' 'retainers', and would perform their bidding (especially as soldiers) in return for clothing, bed and board. The household or 'family' of one 13th-century lord amounted to 200 people, while that of the king would usually be at least twice that size.

Even in the largest palaces, it would not have been possible to provide so many people with individual accommodation, and only the most senior among them could have expected the luxury of a bed and chamber of their own.

A Peasant's Hovel

'Ful sooty was hir bour, and eek hir hall,' says Chaucer of his dairywoman's 'narwe cotage'. In reality, the poor woman would have had nothing so grand as a hall and bower; but neither would she have had a chimney, so her cottage would indeed have been full of smoke.

Right: *Stokesay Castle, Shropshire, built in the 13th century by a wealthy merchant, is a fine example of a fortified manor-house. The great hall is flanked by a defensive tower and, on either side, by living quarters.*

Right: A 15th-century illustration showing the medieval Tower of London brilliantly white-washed. Its central keep is still known as the 'White Tower'. The brightly coloured buildings in the background were also typical of medieval times.

Below: A splendid castle being built. The Normans used their residences as a means of domination and control, inspiring fear and loathing among the peasantry.

Everyone else would have to lay down his pallet on the floor of the great hall or in any other convenient space. Personal servants seem routinely to have slept in the chambers of the lord and his lady (who would always have her own, separate quarters). Privacy was non-existent.

The houses of the medieval peasantry must have been fairly insubstantial, as none has survived intact. Those at Bamburgh in Northumberland were of timber, and could be hastily dismantled and carried into the castle at the threat of a Scottish raid. In other regions, such as the Cotswolds, houses were built of stone; but mostly they were of timber and wattle and daub. Peasant housing typically took the form of a long-house, with accommodation for the family at one end, and a byre for the cattle at the other.

Below: The town-house of a medieval merchant, in French Street, Southampton.

PAINTED HALLS & CHAMBERS

I t is a common misconception that medieval castles and manors were dark, dreary and dank. Unfortunately it is rarely possible to see, or even to imagine these buildings as they once were. The most splendid of them, including the royal palaces of Westminster and Clarendon, have not survived, and those that have are either in ruins or have been modernised to meet the needs of their later occupants.

Both the interior and exterior walls of medieval houses, including those of the peasants, were usually plastered and either whitewashed or coloured with natural pigments, such as ochre (regional peculiarities such as 'Suffolk pink' are with us still). In the wealthier houses, plastered walls were invariably adorned with rich (and expensive) oil-based paints, such as vermilion red or cobalt blue, to create geometrical or floral patterns, or scenes from history, legend or the Bible. In 1246 Henry III had his chambers at Clarendon Palace, near Salisbury, decorated with green-painted wainscot (oak panelling) spangled with gilded stars of lead. In his *aula* or hall, religious scenes were depicted in 'exquisite colours'. These wonders have been mostly obscured or destroyed by later generations. Indeed, the great chamber at Longthorpe Tower, Cambridgeshire, is the only place in England where the elaborate medieval wall paintings are still intact. Parish churches and cathedrals would also have been painted in this way, inside and out, including all the stone-work and statuary.

Above: St Stephen's Throne, in Hereford Cathedral, dates from about 1200. Such 'seats of dignity' were a feature of noble households.

Top: *This battle-scene is typical of medieval decoration.*

Surprisingly, the exterior of a castle is also likely to have been whitewashed, and any wooden structures may well have been brightly painted. With coloured roof-tiles too, and fluttering banners overhead, the genuine medieval castle conformed far more to the fairy-tale image than might be supposed. The Tower of London, for example, was a gleaming spectacle on the edge of the city.

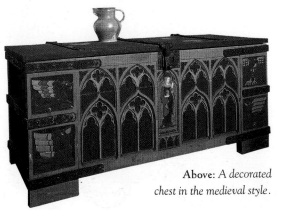

Above: *A decorated chest in the medieval style.*

Right: *Henry III's superb 13th-century door to St George's Chapel, Windsor has original ironwork which bears the signature of the smith, Gilbertus.*

Below: *A 14th-century* Mappa Mundi, *or World* Map, *showing Jerusalem as the centre of the world, where all good Christians hoped to travel.*

Decorative floor-tiles, perhaps with heraldic or other designs, were a common feature; many have been preserved. The ceilings and fireplaces of great houses, as well as the interior shutters which helped to keep out draughts, would also have been richly decorated. From the 13th century onwards it was normal for the windows of a wealthy person's house to be glazed. The skill of glass-making dates back to ancient times, but glass continued to be an expensive luxury in the Middle Ages. There is even evidence of glass being removed from the windows when the master was not in residence. Ideally, this would be painted glass, for stained-glass windows were not restricted to churches and cathedrals but were a much coveted form of decoration in domestic buildings.

A Travelling Household

Lords and ladies in the Middle Ages felt the need to travel constantly between their own scattered estates or in the train of the king, with their household retainers and the rumbling waggons which conveyed their goods and chattels from place to place. Monarchs were the most restless itinerants of all. It was rare for them to stay in any one place for more than a few days, and there were royal castles, palaces, manors and hunting-lodges in every county of England. King John (1199–1216) appears not to have remained anywhere for more than a month throughout his entire reign.

Below: *A travelling-carriage for royal ladies. A procession of waggons conveys the household's goods and chattels, and furnishings.*

COATS OF ARMS

Above: *The arms of Edward III. The blue garter badge and motto, Honi soit qui mal y pense ('Shame on him who thinks ill of it') are said to derive from an incident when the chivalrous king retrieved the fallen garter of his mistress.*

Above: *The arms, from about 1421, of Sir Thomas Beauchamp, Earl of Warwick, on his Garter stall-plate in St George's Chapel, Windsor, are a typical heraldic representation of knightly arms.*

The original 'coats of arms' were part of the costume or equipment of the knights, the designs on which began in the 12th century to be handed down through families. Until the late 13th century, these were military insignia, a distinction of those knights who were, or had been, available for active service; soon, however, they were being used also by the wives and daughters of knights, on their seals or in manuscripts, as marks of identity. In the 14th and 15th centuries, coats of arms came to be generally adopted by non-military members of the gentry and by clerics, as well as by towns and corporations, such as the 'livery companies', or trade guilds, of London.

The original purpose of having simple devices painted on a shield or embroidered on a surcoat is obscure. The most common explanation is that a knight in full armour needed some ready means of identification. This is more likely to have been true at the tournament than on the battlefield, and indeed it was in and around the tournament that 'heraldry', the science of regulating and identifying coats of arms, whose technical language is still based

on Anglo-Norman French, was refined. An equally plausible explanation is that the decorated coat or shield of arms was a mark of status, a symbol of the pride of the individual knight in his rank or kindred and a sign that he was one of the élite. At any rate, heraldry has been one of the most enduring of all medieval inventions, as coats of arms are still in use throughout the world as symbols of family and corporate identity and pride.

Above: *An illustration of Sir Geoffrey Luttrell with his family, showing how heraldry was used in the days of knights-in-armour. Coats of arms were, literally, garments.*

Above: *A modern representation of Richard Neville, Earl of Warwick ('the Kingmaker') based on his equestrian seal. The shield, helm, mantling and crest are still the essential elements of a 'coat of arms'.*

Above: *The Order of the Garter today includes ladies, such as Margaret Thatcher, and men of action like Sir Edmund Hillary, the conqueror of Everest. Here, the Sovereign accompanies them to their annual service.*

Since no two families may bear the same arms, it follows that the simplest and most striking designs were adopted at an early stage and that they are now the mark of very ancient lineage. The member of the Harcourt family who adopted their beautifully plain coat, which consists of two horizontal stripes or bars painted gold (or yellow) on a red background, may simply have highlighted a pair of metal bars which reinforced his shield.

Likewise, it has been suggested that the crescents which adorned many early coats of arms represented actual metal attachments which had been fastened on to the shields as deflectors. In some very rare cases, the distinction of a shield was that it was painted in a single, striking colour, such as the plain red shield of the lords of Albret in south-western France, many of whom were in the service of the Plantagenets.

The Sovereign's Heralds

The heralds' duties were to record and regulate the 'blazon', or technical description, of coats of arms and to organize ceremonial occasions, duties which are still performed today by the heralds of the Royal Household. On special occasions, such as the State Opening of Parliament and the annual service of the Order of the Garter at Windsor Castle, the heralds process in the short-sleeved overcoats or 'tabards' bearing the royal arms that have been their uniform since the Middle Ages.

Above: *The Garter Knights' heraldic banners make a brilliant display in the choir of St George's Chapel, Windsor.*

FEASTS & FESTIVALS

Dining in a great household was a ritual and a pleasure, involving elaborate preparation by an army of servants. Not every meal was as memorable as the wedding-feast of Henry III's daughter Margaret with King Alexander of Scotland in 1251, when the bill for the bread alone amounted to £7,000; or the so-called Feast of the Swans in 1306, held for the newly knighted Edward, Prince of Wales, and his companions, in Westminster Hall. The centre-piece of the meal was a pair of swans, a regal dish, which had been re-dressed in their natural plumage and decorated with gilded nets and reeds, and which were carried into the hall, to great acclaim, by a procession of minstrels.

It was originally the custom to dine in the great hall, which was the centre of life in a medieval castle or manor-house. The king or lord would be seated at the high table on a dais at one end, with a tapestry on the wall behind him. His closest companions and members of his family would sit with him, while the rest of his household would be seated at trestle-tables in the body of the hall.

In polite society it was usual to wash ceremoni-ously before and after each meal. The image of the medieval baron behaving like a brute at the table,

Below: A picture of a royal feast from 1387 shows the 'trenchers', or slices of poor quality bread, used in the Middle Ages instead of plates. The hall is sumptuously decorated. The men wearing conical hats, or 'mitres', are bishops.

Below: A 13th-century picture of a king dining at the high table. He and his companions would occupy one side of the table, enabling the servants, who were of noble rank, to wait on them on bended knee.

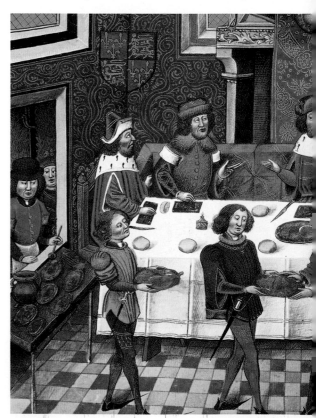

and even throwing bones over his shoulder, is far from the truth. Tables were covered with white cloths and spotless linen was a matter of pride. The staple diet of the well-off was meat of all kinds or, when the Church forbade it, fish, all served with a spicy sauce. The food would be cut up and eaten on a thick, square-cut slice of inferior bread called a 'trencher', which would be shared with a neighbour or 'mess-mate'. In one of the greater houses, a silver platter might be placed beneath the trencher.

People ate with their fingers (forks were not in general use in England until the 17th century). Such intimate eating habits required the observance of strict good manners: no-one should ever dip dirty fingernails into a shared trencher, or talk with his mouth full, or drink from a shared cup with greasy lips. Only a glutton, or 'trencher-man', would actually eat his trencher; they were usually collected up and distributed as alms to the poor.

Opposite, top: Dining al fresco: a hunting-party from the mid-14th century.

Peasants' Fare

The staple diet of peasants consisted of cereals (oats, barley and wheat) eaten in the form of porridge, broths and bread. The poor were rarely fortunate enough to have meat, eggs and fish to eat. Colds and mild fevers often proved fatal to people who were already weakened by a poor diet.

Medieval people would rise at dawn, or even earlier. In great houses, the day would begin and end with a religious service. People might start the day at 5am and dine at 9 or 10 in the morning (breakfast seems to have been uncommon). Supper might be at 5 or 6 in the evening, and everyone would be in bed by 8 or 9pm. Beeswax candles were extremely expensive, so most people had to make do with inefficient tallow candles made from animal fat. It is not surprising that the fullest use was made of the daylight.

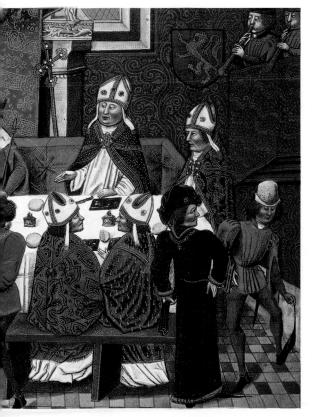

Above: The Great Hall at Winchester Castle was the setting for occasional parliaments and for feasts. The high table was on a dais at one end, while trestle-tables and benches would be set down the length of the room.

MUSIC & MERRYMAKING

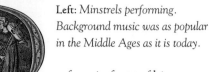

Kings, noblemen, and even the least of the gentry employed minstrels among their household servants, although others were itinerant. Many of these entertainers enjoyed high wages and status. Trumpeters, drummers and fifers were always on hand to attend on a great man and support his dignity. They might play at mealtimes or in the private quarters of the lord, sit up at night for insomniacs, and even provide background music for people who were bathing.

The minstrels were poets, singers and storytellers, as well as musicians. Their most exacting duties were organising and performing at great court functions, such as feast days, royal marriages and knighting ceremonies. At the celebrated Feast of the Swans hosted by Edward I in 1306, an army of minstrels and other performers was on hand to provide the entertainment and organise the ceremonial. On such occasions, the numbers of minstrels would be swelled by travelling performers: acrobats, jugglers, conjurers and tumblers. One of Edward I's favourite performers was the appropriately named Matilda Makejoy, a *saltatrix* or acrobatic dancer, who is believed to have made her vaults in the nude. As Edward also hired her to

Left: Minstrels performing. Background music was as popular in the Middle Ages as it is today.

perform in front of his young sons, this cannot have been regarded as particularly salacious or shocking.

Another rather surprising royal performer was one Roland le Fartere, whose act, inspired by his name, so delighted Henry I that he rewarded him with a house and 99 acres in Suffolk.

Fools and jesters had a no less important place in court life, and could get away with a great deal of satirical comment. It is said that one jester went too far when he compared Henry III with Christ.

Above: *The saltatrix or acrobatic dancer shown here could never have performed her tricks in such heavy clothing. Such dancers usually wore little or nothing. The monk who illustrated this Bible-scene may have added the clothing out of respect, or modesty.*

Above: A medieval lady in her garden. Small corners such as this one were often cultivated within the walls of a castle.

Below: Entertainments in fancy dress were very popular. Even at tournaments the knights might dress up as characters from Arthurian legend. This scene, from about 1390, shows the dance of the wodehouses, mythical creatures of the woods.

Above: Chess was a game much enjoyed by the nobility. Complicated chess problems were sometimes set by the minstrels, and the whole household might be involved in a game, with large stakes placed on the outcome.

This pious king, the builder of Westminster Abbey, but reputed to be a simpleton, was at first delighted by the comparison, until he pressed the jester for an explanation. Christ, he was told, had been as wise when he was born as he was to be at the age of 30; King Henry was also as wise at 30 as he had been as an infant!

A Travelling Play

The oldest popular play to survive from medieval England, the *Interludium de Clerico et Puella* (The Play of the Clerk and the Girl), was preserved on one side of a tiny roll of parchment, small enough to fit inside the pouch of a wandering minstrel. The roll went missing from the British Museum in 1971.

HUNTING & FALCONRY

The most absorbing pastime of all great men, and of many lesser ones, was hunting. The medieval landscape included stretches of primeval forest and wilderness that were still the haunt of wild boar and even wolves. The Norman kings subjected much of the countryside (about a third of England) to a draconian 'forest law', as a means of protecting the game and reserving the best sport for themselves. The forest law made life very difficult for the residents of these areas, since it hampered any activity (such as cutting wood) that tended to harm or disturb the animals. General resentment of the forest law (applied in special courts by 'verderers', who had some grim penalties

Above: A rabbit-hunt using nets. Rabbits were reared in special farms known as warrens.

Above left: A nobleman's magnificent hunting dogs.

at their disposal) was to some extent addressed in the Magna Carta of 1215. Medieval 'forests' that still survive include the New Forest, Sherwood Forest, Windsor Great Park, and Epping Forest, the remnant of a great royal forest that once included the whole of Essex.

Above: A knight and his lady enjoy the hunt.

Opposite, below: *Huntsmen close in for the kill.*

The ground quarry – deer, fox and wild boar – would generally be pursued on horseback with hounds and dispatched by means of a bow and arrow; birds of all kinds were hunted with falcons. Noble ladies participated as fully, and as expertly, in these activities as the men. Indeed, hunting was so central to the lives of lords and ladies that it had a marked impact on the interiors of their houses, as well as being a source of fresh meat. Their halls appear to have teemed with dogs, which were no doubt fed with scraps from the table. Falconry was regarded as a noble art, and the German Emperor Frederick II, King John's brother-in-law, counselled in his treatise on falconry that a man should share his living quarters with his birds to allow them to become familiar with his retainers and not be distracted by them in the field. It was therefore a sign of high rank to be seen with a hawk on one's wrist, even in church. At other times, these birds would be placed on perches around the hall and

A Fatal Arrow

In 1100 King William Rufus was killed, perhaps not accidentally, by an arrow while hunting in the New Forest. The Rufus Stone now marks the spot. The Conqueror's son was a ruthless, brutal king who had many enemies. He fought his barons and seized Church estates to finance his extravagant way of life.

chamber. An account of a traditional hall describes it as 'strewed with marrow bones, full of hawks' perches, hounds, spaniels and terriers ... hung with the fox skins of this and last year's skinning'.

The instinct to hunt was universal and the hated forest laws were often flouted. The earliest story of Robin Hood is set not in the reign of Richard I, as in the later versions, but of Edward I, whose displeasure Robin incurs by hunting his deer in Sherwood Forest. Determined to meet the elusive outlaw, the king allows himself to be ambushed, disguised as an abbot, but astonishes the outlaws by his dignified manner and generosity. No less impressed, the 'abbot' conveys a royal invitation to dine at Nottingham Castle, where he reveals his identity to the outlaws and gladly accepts their pledges of loyalty.

Above: King John (1199–1216) hunting. Kings and noblemen often demonstrated extraordinary devotion to their horses, hounds and falcons.

CHIVALRY & THE TOURNAMENT

The knights were the élite of medieval society, but this did not necessarily assure them of an easy life. A knight's essential practical skills would be acquired only after a long and rigorous training requiring extreme fitness. A famous French knight of the Hundred Years War, the Marshal Boucicaut, was able, in full armour, to vault on to his horse and even to turn a somersault. A knight was then expected restlessly to seek out adventures and to prove his worth; hence the impulse that many felt to fight the Crusade. He must give constant proof of his loyalty, courage, prowess and hardiness. This last virtue was amply demonstrated by Edward I. On the eve of the battle of Falkirk, old age did not prevent him from sleeping in the open with his men. During the night, his horse rolled on top of him and he suffered broken ribs; yet he proceeded to win a great victory the following day.

A no less important knightly virtue, however, was *courtoisie*, a grasp of the manners that were appropriate in increasingly refined and sophisticated court circles. An ideal knight was immaculately turned out, graceful in his movements, and highly cultured. His was an intellectual as much as

Right: *These 14th-century effigies in Chichester Cathedral are probably of Richard Fitzalan, Earl of Arundel, and his wife. It seems that their hands may have been joined by a 19th-century restorer.*

Above: *Chivalrous knights and fair ladies, in a romantic portrayal of a classic tournament scene.*

a physical calling, in which a ready wit, eloquence in speech, and even musical accomplishments were highly prized. Some of the leading lawyers of medieval England were also active knights. The games of chess and backgammon were other intellectual and social pursuits at which they were expected to shine.

The chivalrous knight should also take care of the poor and defenceless, and, to all comers, show open-handed *largesse* or generosity. It was often, if not always, the recognition of fair ladies that he sought in his quests. This was particularly true at the tournament, the sometimes extremely violent contest of military skills that was considered an essential preparation for real warfare. Battles, tournaments and love affairs were, then, the passionate pursuits of many: but the poor, landless knight or younger son, who had to earn his keep precariously in the retinue of a greater man, might also be motivated by the need to make money. That end was most easily achieved through royal favour, through marriage to a rich heiress, or through the prize and ransom money that might be won in a war or at the tournament.

Courtly Love

The art of courtly love was pioneered by the Plantagenets' 12th-century ancestor Duke William IX of Aquitaine, 'the first of the troubadours'. The expressions of romantic passion and courtesy in the songs of the troubadours, and their placing of women on a pedestal, were revolutionary and have had a lasting effect on Western culture, in such diverse areas as manners and popular music.

Right: A knight accepts the favours of his lady. He might hope to win her approval by distinguishing himself in combat. A knight would not normally have been in love with his own wife but would have married her for her property.

Below: A scene from a tournament, which took place in London, evoking all the colour and pageantry of such occasions, although fatalities were not uncommon and sometimes included members of the royal family.

LIFE & DEATH IN THE TOWNS

S ociety in the Middle Ages was predominantly rural, with only about five per cent of the population living in towns. Medieval cities were tiny by modern standards. London had around 50,000 inhabitants; York, its nearest rival, fewer than 8,000. Typically, the boundaries of both these cities were marked by impressive walls. These are largely preserved at York, while those which once enclosed the 'square mile' of London (for this was the entire extent of the medieval city) are remembered in street names such as Ludgate, Aldgate, Bishopsgate and indeed, London Wall.

Towns usually developed because they were convenient market-places or administrative centres. The weekly market was the focus of retail trade and a major event in people's lives, since there were no shops or stores as we know them. The quarters of towns or cities that were assigned to particular tradesmen, such as the Shambles (or

Above: *The so-called Jew's House in Lincoln was built in the late 12th century by a wealthy townsman, who was not necessarily a Jew.*

Below: *The King's School, Canterbury, dates from the 6th century and is England's oldest public school. An education here opened up, for peasant boys, the opportunity of a distinguished career in the Church.*

Above: *Traitors such as Hugh Despenser faced the worst punishment, of being hanged, drawn and quartered.*

Below: *A physician tends his patients.*

The Black Death

Efficient trade routes extending as far as China were to prove a severe disadvantage in 1348 when rats carrying the bubonic plague spread the Black Death rapidly throughout Europe, wiping out as much as one-third of the population. Entire villages were permanently abandoned. In densely packed towns such as Bristol and Winchester the death toll was as high as fifty per cent.

Below: Queen Anne, wife of Richard II, died of the plague in 1394.

'slaughter-houses') at York, were usually where they lived and had their workshops. The streets of the medieval town were invariably narrow and dirty, with open drains, and the houses mostly wooden, with thatched roofs. Yet, where they survive, substantial stone houses are evidence of the fortunes that were to be made there, not least from the wool trade.

The towns were also the centres of education. A well brought-up person would have had at least

some instruction in French, the main language of business, government and culture. From the 12th century, increasing numbers of people were taught to read, from Latin grammars. In the face of growing government bureaucracy, literacy had ceased to be the almost exclusive preserve of the clergy, and by the 13th century was a skill that seems to have been enjoyed by men and women of all classes.

This was true of increasing numbers of peasants, as well as gentry. The peasant is likely to have gained his education from his parish priest, who had a duty under Canon Law to provide all the children in his flock with a free education.

COSTUME & ARMOUR

Throughout most of the Middle Ages, men and women of all classes wore identical woollen dresses, hose (thigh-length stockings), and fur-lined hoods and mantles (cloaks), which varied only in their quality and cost.

The *braies*, or underwear worn by men (similar to a loin-cloth), would support the obligatory hose by means of ties. Although all western Europeans wore dresses (or tunics), the outfit was considered incomplete without hose. A contingent of bare-legged Scots were the cause of consternation in 1096 when they joined the armies assembling in France to fight the First Crusade.

Everyone wore a linen chemise or undershirt which would correspond in length and shape to the tunic. Any number of short-sleeved or sleeve-less super-tunics, usually of a different colour and material, would be worn over the tunic for effect, or to provide additional

Right: *Peasants harvesting. Working-men typically wore their tunics short.*

Below: *The 13th-century effigy of Robert, Duke of Normandy, in Gloucester Cathedral. His* hauberk, *or shirt of mail, is clearly shown, as are his* coif *(cap), sleeves, gauntlets and leggings of mail.*

warmth. Bright colours, silks and satins were worn only by the rich. Similarly, while the mantles and hoods of the poor would be lined with rabbit-fur or sheepskin, the wealthy would be swathed in ermine or vair. Vair is a variegated fur made from the grey-blue and white pelts of the Baltic squirrel, and was an enormously costly import. Hundreds or even thousands of these pelts were needed to line a single cloak.

Fashionable men wore their hair long and elab-orately curled with the aid of perfumed pomades and rollers. A story of the 12th-century Duke William IX of Aquitaine, an ancestor of the

Below: *By the 15th century mail had given way to plate armour, as illustrated by this effigy of Richard Neville, Earl of Warwick, in St Mary's Church, Warwick.*

Right: *The Beauchamp tomb in Worcester Cathedral, showing a knight wearing his 'coat of arms', and the typical costume of a lady.*

Above: *Ermine and vair are common in heraldry, as, here, in the arms of Brittany and Ferrers. Ermine-lined robes are still worn by peers on formal occasions, such as the annual State Opening of Parliament. Hairs from the heels of black lambs are stitched on to the stoat's white winter coat.*

Plantagenets, tells how he was instructed by a bald bishop, on pain of excommunication, to give up his mistress. The duke laughed at him and said that he would give her up on the day he saw the bishop in curlers.

Clothing, or at least the underwear, was evidently laundered regularly. Laundresses were the only women whom Richard the Lionheart would allow to accompany his Crusade in 1191. Woollen clothes, when dirty, could be sent back to the cloth merchant and re-shorn to expose a fresh surface; but the medieval equivalent of dry-cleaning would have been beyond the means of most people.

The retainers of kings and noblemen would receive payments in clothing, or livery, in addition to their regular wages. The biannual issue of robes or tunics in the household of Edward I (1272–1307) was equivalent to a payment of 20 shillings. The average peasant survived on little more than this sum for the entire year. The code of chivalry impelled noblemen and women, who were like modern millionaires, to share their good fortune with others through displays of extravagant *largesse*. William the Marshal, Earl of Pembroke (d. 1219), usually distributed over 80 fine robes among his household knights at Pentecost, an observance he regarded as a matter of honour.

Left: *Portrait of a king, believed to be Edward I, in Westminster Abbey. The linen undershirt, expensive overgarments, jewellery and fashionable hairstyle of a 13th-century king are clearly shown.*

PLACES TO VISIT

Britain's medieval heritage is deservedly famous. Below are listed just some of the sights not to be missed on a tour of 'medieval' England.

Arundel Castle, West Sussex: A classic motte and bailey castle, still held by the descendants (the Dukes of Norfolk) of its medieval owners.

Canterbury: The cathedral, with its shrine to St Thomas Becket, was the most popular destination for pilgrims in medieval England. The King's School is England's oldest public school.

The British Library, London: The library displays selections from its wonderful collection of medieval illuminated manuscripts, such as Matthew Paris's 13th- century sketch of an elephant.

The British Museum, The Victoria and Albert Museum, London and the Burrell Collection, Glasgow: These museums preserve splendid medieval artefacts, including painted chests, stained-glass windows, floor-tiles and ornaments.

Chester: A beautiful city with many medieval buildings, including the cathedral and parts of the boundary walls.

Corfe Castle, Dorset: Royal castle on a majestic site; though it was deliberately ruined in the 17th century, enough features remain to conjure up its medieval splendour.

English Heritage sites: These include Dover Castle, Kent, Framlingham Castle, Suffolk, Kenilworth Castle, Warwickshire, Ludlow Castle and Stokesay Castle, Shropshire, and Portchester Castle, Hampshire.

Glastonbury Abbey, Somerset: Exceptionally well-preserved ruins, on a site steeped in legend, of one of medieval England's wealthiest abbeys.

Hereford Cathedral: Includes a celebrated *Mappa Mundi* (world map), medieval tombs and St Stephen's Throne, a classic nobleman's chair.

Lincoln: City with a fine medieval cathedral and buildings, including 'The Jew's House' (15 The Strait) built by a wealthy citizen.

The New Forest, Hampshire, Sherwood Forest, Nottinghamshire, Windsor Great Park, Berkshire, Epping Forest, Essex: Hunting reserves of the medieval kings. See where royal game was poached by outlaws such as the legendary Robin Hood.

Oxford: Home of England's oldest university, with many medieval colleges, including Christ Church and Merton.

Rievaulx Abbey (English Heritage) and Fountains Abbey (National Trust), North Yorkshire: The impressive remains of two mighty Cistercian monasteries, where rigidly disciplined monks created model estates.